FACILITATION GUIDE FOR

TOOLS TO CHANGE THE WORLD

STUDY GUIDE BASED ON THE
PROGRESSIVE UTILIZATION THEORY (PROUT)
LEVEL 1

Dada Maheshvarananda and Mirra Price, M. Ed., Ed.M.

PROUTIST UNIVERSAL
COPENHAGEN

Publisher's Cataloging-in-Publication data

Names: Maheshvarananda, Dada, author. | Price, Mirra, author.
Title: Facilitation guide for tools to change the world : study guide based on the Progressive Utilization Theory (Prout) , level 1 / Dada Maheshvarananda and Mirra Price, M. Ed., Ed.M.
Description: Includes index. | Copenhagen, Denmark: Proutist Universal, 2018
Identifiers: ISBN 978-87-89552-01-9
Subjects: LCSH Prout (Economic theory) | Prout (Economic theory)--Study guides. | Sarkar, Prabhat Ranjan, 1921-1990. | Economics--Philosophy. | Economics--Religious aspects. | Economics--Sociological aspects. | Economics--Moral and ethical aspects. | Monetary policy. | BISAC POLITICAL SCIENCE / Public Policy / Economic Policy | POLITICAL SCIENCE / Political Ideologies / Communism, Post-Communism & Socialism | BUSINESS & ECONOMICS / Business Ethics
Classification: LCC HB72 .M233 2019 | DDC 330.12--dc23

Contents

FACILITATION NOTES
(Excerpted From The Manual Introduction)

Each module is designed to last a little more than two hours. This study guide can be used in at least six ways:

1. A group can meet weekly for two-and-a-half hour sessions for 10 weeks.
2. A group can meet for two intense weekends (10 hours each weekend).
3. It can be used as a five-day intensive training course.
4. It can be used as remote video conferencing for two-and-a-half hour sessions for 10 weeks with learners scattered in different locations (using a program like Zoom).
5. The content can be filmed to make an online distance learning course available for people to take at their convenience (with no discussion).
6. The manual can be read like a book (with no discussion).

Organizing a Study Circle

Some study groups fail because they are conducted poorly, with unfocused discussions and a few dominant voices. Other groups end after a few weeks because the participants are only studying; they're not *doing anything*. Rev. Martin Luther King, Jr. called this "paralysis of analysis," forever studying the issues and never acting. To avoid these problems, *Tools to Change the World: Level 1* is designed to be democratic, and to encourage real sharing. It inspires participants to start concrete work that will lead to a more just world society.

Group Size and Mix: We hope that everyone who likes this manual will feel confident enough to organize study circles. Invite friends, colleagues, and members of organizations you belong to. Use social media like Facebook and Meetup, and post flyers at strategic places in your neighborhood.

Generally, the best size for a study circle group is about 10. Ten members are enough to take on practical duties and to provide enough diversity to have good discussions. A group with fewer than eight members places an overly large burden on each person, especially if some people drop out over time. On the other hand, it is very difficult to have a discussion in too large of a group. With more than 17 people, it is best to split into two separate groups.

This study guide is geared toward adults. Some high school students are mature enough to engage with these concepts and ideas, but younger people typically are not.

How Much Time for Each Module? Most groups meet once a week. This works well and helps the group maintain focus and momentum. A group focused more intensely on study, such as a college class, might meet twice a week. Other groups, with members who have many other commitments, might decide to meet less often. However, we recommend that you meet at least twice a month so that the group maintains cohesion and members do not lose track of ideas from earlier sessions.

We realize that sessions shorter than two-and-a-half hours may work better for some people and that longer sessions may be tiring. However, anything less than two-and-a-half hours will make the group feel rushed, will reduce the quantity and quality of discussion, and will make the exercises impractical. We encourage groups to have a short break in longer sessions.

Meeting Place: A good meeting place is one that is easy to find and travel to, and large enough with enough chairs for everyone. It should also be private and quiet, so members can speak freely and without distraction.

Set the chairs up in a rough circle so everyone can see one another. Have a large easel (or a chair and a board set up as an easel), blackboard, whiteboard, or a blank wall where the group can record notes on large pieces of paper ("wall charts"). Or you can use a laptop computer and a projector.

The living room in a private home, or a meeting room at a library, church, community center, or labor hall are all good places. Restaurants, bars, and social clubs are usually noisy and distracting. If you meet at a member's home, you may want to change to a different house each session so that no one person is burdened by hosting the group repeatedly.

Punctuality: Start each session on time and end on time. If people come late, they will miss out. The initial activities of each module are designed to function well even if some members have not yet arrived. Don't punish those who arrive on time by forcing them to wait for latecomers. Close on time, too, so that participants can get to their next appointments on time.

Expectations: Study circles work well when participants commit to the process and to the other members. Each person should agree to:

Try their best to attend all ten sessions for the full time (two-and-a-half hours each).

Read the assigned module before each session.

Participate honestly in discussions and exercises.

Work with others cooperatively.

Sometimes accept an additional role as facilitator, timekeeper, etc.

Do as many additional readings and viewings as possible.

Do as many activities as possible.

Deliver good, succinct presentations to the group.

Despite people's best intentions, events sometimes prevent them from fulfilling all their commitments. Still, *Tools to Change the World* is important. By committing to this challenge to learn and use these tools, the course stays relevant, interesting, inspiring, and fun.

In Which Country and Year Do You Live? Both the authors of this Study Guide are in the United States, so most of the examples and supporting statistics are from there. We used the most current data we could find in 2018. We strongly encourage facilitators to look up relevant current data in each module from your region and country.

The Design of Each Module

Excitement Sharing (): "What is something good that has happened in your life since we last met? Or would anyone like to read from your journal or share your recent activities?" The first module explains journaling as an activist tool. Indirectly, it encourages note-taking. More importantly, it causes everyone to reflect on the ideas and tools of the course outside of the meetings. Everyone does not have to say something in Excitement Sharing every week. This section should be limited to 5-10 minutes.

The Social Reality: This is a short five-minute presentation about a particular social problem in our world, such as poverty, hunger, unemployment, debt, crime and corruption, pollution and climate change, etc.

The Social Reality Discussion Question (): Then each person takes a minute to express how the problem directly or indirectly impacts her or him. The facilitator concludes by saying, "Excuse me, please, but we're going to end this discussion now because, as usual in this course, we want to focus on the solutions." (10 minutes).

Cooperative Game (): These are team-building exercises that create powerful, safe learning experiences. Cooperative games help participants interact and share, gain self confidence, improve collaboration, and develop genuine compassion for others. As Bill Ayers said, these are "cooperative calisthenics, little exercises to prepare us for the huge changes that are essential to our survival on this earth" (Maheshvarananda 2017, 1). (Bill Ayers is a social justice organizer and activist, a teacher and former Distinguished Professor of Education at the University of Illinois at Chicago; in the 1960s he co-founded the radical Weather Underground.) (10-15 minutes).

Prout's Vision: The analysis and vision of Prout are powerful tools for changing the world. Social problems are inter-connected and caused by an exploitative global economic system. The fundamentals of Prout help us understand the root causes of social and economic problems. Prout's Vision for a better way to organize the economy, government, medicine, agriculture, education, the workplace, and other fields clarifies not only what we're against, but even more importantly, what we stand for. (20 minutes).

Discussion Questions (): After the presentation, the group can discuss some of the questions. There is no need to discuss them all—different people will find some questions more interesting than others. The facilitator can also ask different questions. There are no right or wrong answers. The questions prompt participants to think about the ideas in the module, and so each reply will be, by definition, their honest opinion. One way to do this is to go around the group, allowing each person a chance to answer, and starting with a different person each time. Explain that anyone can pass if they want more time to think, and also can give their opinion at the end if they think of something later. Only after everyone has answered, will people be allowed to speak again.

Activist Tools: "Philosophers have only interpreted the world, in various ways. The point, however, is to change it." - Karl Marx. The twelve activist tools included in this manual are proven techniques that unlock our capacity to educate, to build collective power and to make change. Grassroots community organizing skills are mighty arms, even when the wealthy and powerful oppose us. Learning and practicing these activist tools empower us to do something concrete.

Activist Tool Exercise (): The activist skills include an exercise to practice using the tool together.

Self Reflection (): At the end of each module, the facilitator answers the question, "How do you feel you did?" After answering, he or she has the option of asking the other members to also give constructive feedback.

Written Feedback (): Written anonymous feedback forms are also very helpful. Ask participants to fill them out on the spot before they leave, while the experience is still fresh in their minds.

Activities: There are further activities, some of which involve community research projects, showing how the Prout Vision applies to your situation. The more activities that you do, alone or in groups, the more engaged you will become.

Further Readings and Viewings: These are articles and videos freely available on the Internet that participants can access in order to further their learning experience.

Democratic Group Process

The Progressive Utilization Theory is comprehensive, addressing politics, economics, culture, history, psychology, and much more. Its founder, Prabhat Ranjan Sarkar, dictated approximately 1,500 pages on Prout. Because of the breadth of the material, few people feel confident to teach it. Many people have learned a little and like what they find, yet always look for an experienced Proutist to lead any discussion about Prout. If none is available, Prout discussions do not take place.

To overcome this difficulty, *Tools to Change the World* is designed to empower anyone to start a democratic study group. As the great Brazilian revolutionary educator Paulo Freire insisted, we all have different kinds of knowledge, so by sharing, we will always learn.

To keep the group on track while preventing anyone from dominating the discussion or decision-making, the participants should take on the following roles in rotation:

Convener and Host: This is the one who starts the Study Circle and recruits participants. They arrange the logistics of the first meeting, arrange child care, welcome everyone when they arrive, and usually facilitate that first meeting to show the group how it's done. Afterwards the role of host can also rotate.

Facilitator: Each week a different participant will be encouraged to prepare and present, in his or her own words, the material for the following module. The facilitator should:

Plan: With the assistant facilitator, develop a meeting agenda. Set time limits for each item, based on this study guide, the desires of the group, and feedback from the previous meeting. Before the meeting, display the agenda with time limits on a large wall chart in the meeting room.

Start and end the meeting on time.

Apply Agreements: At the beginning of the meeting, review the agenda and time limits with the group. Make any changes the group desires and agrees on together. Throughout the meeting, keep the group on task. Suggest when it is appropriate to move on to the next agenda item. If the group expresses a desire to change the agenda, help the group make a new agreement, and then enforce it.

Guide: Introduce each agenda item or ask someone else to do so. Remind the group when they have strayed from the agenda, perhaps by asking if they want to return. Keep reports, discussion, and brainstorming sessions within agreed-upon time limits.

Encourage: Help everyone share in the discussion. Be sensitive to reserved people being cut off or intimidated by more outgoing folks. Encourage those who have not participated much to speak more and encourage those who talk a lot to listen more and speak less. Help the other members of the group who have taken on roles to do their jobs.

Monitor: Be sensitive to the feelings of the group members. Note expressions of emotion or uneasiness, which may indicate that some change in the process is needed.

Reveal: Try to get important but unspoken frustrations, needs, fears, expectations, etc., out in the open so they can be dealt with directly and with respect. "Hidden agendas" are often an important source of failure and frustration in groups.

Summarize at times what has been said including disagreements, and ask the group, "Is that accurate?" This reassures people that they have been heard.

Sort: Suggest ways to separate unlike ideas and group together similar ideas. Point out agreements and disagreements.

Synthesize: Suggest ways that solutions or ideas can be melded together. Different approaches may reinforce one another.

<u>Suggest Directions</u>: Focus the discussion by suggesting a particular order. Begin with one item, and then proceed to others.

<u>Mediate</u>: When people seem unable to hear each other, ask them to repeat in their own words what they think they heard. Then ask if the speaker felt it was an accurate re-statement of what they meant. If not, invite the person to rephrase the idea until everyone understands.

Assistant Facilitator: This person assists the facilitator in all duties and is the backup if the facilitator is unable to come. Typically, the assistant facilitator will become facilitator for the next module.

Timekeeper: This is a crucial, yet delicate role. No one likes to be interrupted when they are speaking. When an engaging discussion or an exciting activity is underway, participants will naturally want to continue. The timekeeper should give people a minute or two of warning, mainly during reports, so that they can use the rest of their time wisely. The role of the timekeeper is to gently remind the speaker or the group when the allotted time is over, and to ask if the group wants an extension. If the consensus is yes, the timekeeper should either suggest ten more minutes or ask the group how much longer they want to spend on this discussion.

Recorder: This person writes notes on the wall chart when it is useful to the group. This may include recording agenda changes, important facts or ideas mentioned in reports, brainstormed ideas for action, ideas proposed in the evaluation section, etc. Despite the best efforts of the recorder, it is sometimes difficult to recognize important ideas that should be recorded as they come up. So it is useful to have a separate piece of paper posted to the side where anyone can record thoughts if she or he feels the need.

MODULE 1: THE RIGHT TO LIVE

Objectives of Module 1

1. To understand how poverty impacts people and affects their right to live a full life.
2. To realize the power of guaranteeing the basics of life to everyone.
3. To understand the strengths and weaknesses of Karl Marx's work.
4. To learn how to tell your story in a clear, compelling and inspiring way.
5. To understand the power of journaling and to begin a journal.

The Social Reality Discussion Question Poverty

Our question now is: Can you share a personal experience of poverty? Are you or have you ever been poor? How does seeing poverty make you feel?

We will go around the room, and ask everyone to say their name, briefly what your experience with poverty was, and how it made you feel. Please speak for just one minute each.

[After everyone has spoken, 10-15 minutes] Excuse me, please, but we're going to end this discussion now, only because, as usual in this course, we want to focus on the solutions.

Cooperative Game - Interviews

Sit with someone you don't know. Imagine you are an activist journalist. Ask your partner the following four questions and remember their answers. Then your partner will ask you the same questions: 1.) What is your name? 2.) Where are you from? 3.) What in your opinion is the biggest problem in your country? 4.) What is your personal motto? In other words, if you were to print something on a T-shirt, what would it say? You have 10 minutes. At the end you will each introduce your partner to the group, telling the group their answers to the questions. (15 minutes.)

Prout's Vision Discussion Questions

What would be the benefits if no one in the world worried about getting enough money to buy food, clothes, housing, education, and medical care for his or her family? What do you think it would it be like?

Do you think it is possible to find work for everyone? Consider child care, mentoring young people, caring for the elderly, teaching preventive health care to everyone, installing wind and solar energy everywhere, building electric vehicles and better public transport to replace all gasoline-driven vehicles, improving infrastructure, environmental cleanup and reforestation, and growing food for local markets.

"From each according to his ability, to each according to his need." What do you think about this concept?

What are the strengths and weaknesses of Karl Marx's ideas?

Activist Tool Exercise Practicing Your Story of Self

The first goal of this exercise is to begin learning how to tell your personal story of why you feel called to help build a better world. The second goal is to begin learning how to coach others by listening carefully, offering feedback, asking questions, etc. In this way you can develop leadership in others, as well as in yourself. Be prepared to take some risks, and support your team members as they take risks, too.

Divide into groups of four to seven. Select a timekeeper for each group. Spend five minutes for everyone to silently develop your "story of self." Choose one event, one place, or one important relationship. Take some time to think about the challenge, your choice, and the outcome in your story. Ideally your story reflects the values that brought you here. The outcome might also be something you learned. Experiences to consider: your parents, childhood, adolescence, school, community, role models, career, partner, family, hobbies, interests, talents, experiences, finding passion, overcoming challenges, your first organizing experience, your first awareness about social justice or the environment, or a key moment in nature.

Tell your story to your team members for two to three minutes. The timekeeper needs to hold up three fingers during the first minute, two fingers all during the second minute, one finger during the last minute, and then a "zero" to indicate time is up. This is important to help the speakers pace themselves. Make sure your timekeeper cuts you off. This encourages focus and ensures that everyone has a chance.

After each speaker, the group has three minutes to offer feedback. As before, the timekeeper enforces the limit. Finally the group should choose one speaker to share their story with everyone.

How to Coach and Evaluate Other Stories:
First say what works in the story, focusing on specifics.
Identify the challenge, the choice, and the outcome in the story.
Identify what hope the story can give us.
Clarify key moments when one thing happened instead of another.
Connect the dots in the narrative, showing how someone got from here to there.
Look for themes.
Ask questions about who the intended audience would be and what action or response the speaker wants the audience to do.
Don't offer vague, abstract "feel good" comments. A story teller who is told, "You did a great job", won't know how to improve. Instead try to be very specific about how different parts of the story made you feel.
Don't make value judgments about the storyteller's manner or whether the point they want to make is valid. The key here is that people find ways to express themselves in their own voice—word choice, humor, metaphor, etc. They need to know if the choices they've made communicate their message.
Don't think about what you're going to say in your story while someone else is telling theirs. Listen to the stories of others so you can help them with their efforts; then you can expect the same help from them when it's your turn.
Don't underestimate the power of someone's story. If it doesn't "work" for you, think about why it doesn't, and more importantly, why it might work for someone else.

Closure

The facilitator answers the question, "How do you feel you did?" Confirm the date, time, and place of the next meeting. Ask everyone to read the next module in the manual before the next meeting. Choose roles for the next meeting: host, facilitator, assistant facilitator, timekeeper, and recorder; make sure the facilitator and assistant facilitator have a copy of the Facilitation Guide to prepare Ask participants to write anonymous feedback about the session before they leave. They can use the following Feedback Form, or write whatever they like.

Feedback Form

FEEDBACK – MODULE ___

Please rate each part: 1- excellent, 2- very good, 3- OK, 4- needs much improvement

_____ The venue
_____ Introduction
_____ Social Reality Discussion
_____ Prout's Vision Presentation
_____ Prout's Vision Discussion
_____ Activist Skills Presentation
_____ Activist Skills Exercise
_____ Closure

What did you like best?

What was hardest for you?

Suggestions?

Would you recommend this course to a friend? Why or why not?

MODULE 2: A HOLISTIC PERSPECTIVE

Objectives of Module 2

1. To understand the nature of depression and chronic stress and how it impacts people.
2. To understand the concept of Dharma and the power of an ecological and spiritual outlook.
3. To understand the problems caused by materialism.
4. To realize the power of holistic health and lifestyle changes.
5. To understand the power of meditation and how to practice it.

Excitement Sharing

"What is something good that has happened in your life since we last met? Or would anyone like to read from your journal or share your recent activities?"

The Social Reality Discussion Question Depression, Chronic Stress, and Poor Health

Our question now is: Have you ever known someone who was or is anxious, depressed, or over-stressed? Have you ever known anyone who committed suicide or wanted to commit suicide? How did those experiences impact you? How did it make you feel?

We will go around the room, and ask everyone to say your name, briefly describe what your experiences with depression, stress, and suicide have been, and how they made you feel. As always, anyone may choose to pass. Please speak for just one minute each.

[After everyone has spoken, 10-15 minutes] Excuse me, please, but we're going to stop this discussion now, because, as usual in this course, we want to focus on the solutions.

Cooperative Game - Car-Car

"Trust and responsibility are two very important qualities in creating world peace. This activity will help you experience how you feel about trust and responsibility. The game is called Car-Car, and it's very simple. Let me demonstrate. First I need a volunteer. My partner stands in front of me and is the 'car.' Every car has protective bumpers in front, so please hold your hands in front of your chest with your palms facing outward as your 'bumpers' to protect you in case of any accident. Cars cannot see, so please close your eyes. I am 'the driver', with eyes open. I stand behind the car with my hands on your shoulders and slowly guide you forward. Cars can go in reverse, too. This is a silent activity, so no talking." Demonstrate slow, compassionate driving with your volunteer. "Remember that your partner is going to be nervous, so please move slowly. Are there any questions?"

Then ask everyone to form pairs. If there is an extra person, then you can be their partner. "Remember no talking. OK? Begin!" Quiet music is ideal for this. After 3-4 minutes say, "Stop. Open your eyes, and now switch roles with your partner. OK? Begin!"

At the end, ask everyone to sit or stand with their partner for a couple of minutes and talk about how they felt in both roles, as the car and as the driver. You could then sit or stand in a circle. Ask the group: Did everyone act responsibly toward others in this game?

Trust means to feel safe with, confident in and supported by the group. Do you feel trust in this group? (This debriefing of the event is a very important part of the learning process. 20 minutes)

Prout's Vision Discussion Questions

"You wouldn't tell someone with cancer to 'just get over it.' It may not be cancer, but depression is not weakness, laziness, self-pity, or a choice." What do you think about this?

Have you ever made a change in your lifestyle that improved your health? If so, what change did you make and what happened as a result?

According to *Forbes*, pharmaceutical corporations are the most profitable industries in the world today. What is your opinion about this fact?

Does your government have a strong ecological and spiritual perspective? What are some things that might be different if it did?

"The land does not belong to me; I belong to the land." What is your opinion of this idea?

Have you ever felt an ecological connection with all living things? Have you ever felt a spiritual connection? If so, what was it like?

"There is in the living being a thirst for limitlessness." Do you agree with this? Have you ever experienced it?

Does materialism bother you? Why or why not?

Have you ever practiced meditation? What was your experience?

Have you ever gone outside for a walk to improve your mood? Did a connection with nature help? Why?

Have you been a part of a support group? What was your experience?

The Activist Tool Exercise for Module 2, "An Introduction to Mantra Meditation," is included in the manual.

Closure

The facilitator answers the question, "How do you feel you did?" Confirm the date, time, and place of the next meeting. Ask everyone to read the next module in the manual before the next meeting. Choose roles for the next meeting: host, facilitator, assistant facilitator, timekeeper, and recorder; make sure the facilitator and assistant facilitator have a copy of the Facilitation Guide to prepare. Ask participants to write anonymous feedback about the session before they leave. They can use the Feedback Form at the end of Module 1, or write whatever they like.

MODULE 3: THE WEALTH CAP

Objectives of Module 3

To understand the nature of wealth inequality and how it impacts people.
To realize the power of a cap on wealth.
To understand the power of public speaking and to practice it.

Excitement Sharing

"What is something good that has happened in your life since we last met? Or would anyone like to read from your journal or share your recent activities?"

The Social Reality Discussion Question Wealth Inequality

Our question now is: What is your opinion of income, wealth, and land disparity? How does it impact you? How does it make you feel?

We will go around the room, and ask everyone to say briefly what your opinion is of income, wealth, and land disparity, and how it makes you feel. Please speak for just one minute each.

[After everyone has spoken, 10-15 minutes] Excuse me, please, but we're going to stop this discussion now, only because, as usual in this course, we want to focus on the solutions.

Cooperative Game - How Much Money is Enough?

Read the following instructions: "Planet Earth is limited. Human desires are not.

"The book, *The Spirit Level: Why More Equal Societies Almost Always Do Better* (Wilkinson and Pickett 2009) reveals how inequality has very negative effects on societies: eroding trust, increasing anxiety and illness, and promoting excessive consumption. In countries with high rates of income inequality, each of the following indices are much worse: physical health, mental health, drug abuse, education, imprisonment, obesity, social mobility, trust and community life, violence, teenage pregnancies, and child well-being. Even wealthy people tend to be happier when they live in societies where there is less of a gap between the rich and poor.

"A higher salary may induce a person to work harder or to improve his or her skills to be more productive... to a point. However, there is a limit to the output any one person can achieve: personal capacity is limited, and there are only 24 hours in a day. Production may increase with more money up to a point, but cannot increase indefinitely.

"Inevitably the production curve levels off. After that peak, more incentives will not increase a person's productivity. Offering a salary increase that is a hundred times higher cannot induce one to work a hundred times harder or to become a hundred times more efficient.

"Sit in small groups of about four people and answer the following five discussion questions. One person in each group should take notes.

1. What motivates you to be creative and productive? Consider hope for a better future; your co-workers; your boss; the chance to use your skills, talents, and training; a noble cause; or a higher salary.

2. Have you ever turned down an opportunity to make more money? If so, why? Consider the career you chose, family priorities, something illegal or immoral you heard about, or another job far away.

3. Have you ever known anyone who became less happy when they got more money? How and why did that happen?

4. An ancient yoga saying is: 'Poor is the person with many desires, and rich is the one with no desires.' In your experience is this true?

5. How much money do you think is enough?"

After each group has shared its report, ask the group: There is a slogan, "Money is a human invention—we can change the rules!" Would you agree with this?

An ancient wisdom says, "Be careful what you wish for in life, because it might just happen and not make you any happier." Have you ever experienced this? (20 minutes)

Prout Vision Discussion Questions

All government employees have pay scales. The U.S. federal government pays the president a little more than 10 times the salary of a starting worker, while Norway pays 5.3 times more. Do you think it is reasonable to ask the same from private business?

"Healthy individuals contribute to a healthy society, and a healthy society fosters the development of healthy individuals." Do you agree with this statement, and that individual interests and collective interests do not have to be in conflict?

Mark Friedman lists eight factors that motivate people to work productively: individual ability, personality, the demands of the organization, education, experience, work environment, service culture, and income. What factors motivate you to work hard?

How do you think providing jobs to all with an adequate salary to purchase the minimum necessities would affect the wealth gap?

What do you think is a reasonable cap on wealth? How would you determine this?

Activist Tools Exercise Give a Speech

Each participant chooses a topic from the first three modules on which to speak. Here is a list of possible speech topics:

1. Why is the growing gap between the rich and the poor a problem?
2. Would a cap on wealth be a good thing?
3. Why should economists have an ecological and spiritual perspective?
4. What's wrong with materialism?
5. Can dharma give meaning to one's life?
6. What can we do against the epidemic of depression?
7. What would happen if we guaranteed the minimum necessities of life to everyone?
8. Should products imported from other countries be taxed (tariffs)?
9. Should the minimum wage be increased?
10. Should there be stricter laws to protect endangered species?

11. How is pollution negatively affecting humanity?

12. Do we need to invest more in alternative fuels?

13. Should we have capital punishment?

14. Why is it wrong for the media to promote a certain beauty standard?

15. Should women always be paid the same as men when they do the same work?

16. Is capitalism working in this country?

Write a two to three minute speech. Fifteen minutes will be given to prepare the speeches. Then the speeches will be presented to the whole group. A timekeeper will give a one-minute signal, a two-minute signal, and a 30 second warning. Finally, after three minutes, the timekeeper will make a sound and the speaker must stop. Everyone will write an evaluation of all speeches and give the evaluations to the speaker after their speeches. The evaluations should answer:

1. What strong points does the speaker already have?

2. Did the topic engage you?

3. Did the speech reflect adequate preparation?

4. Did the speaker speak clearly and loudly enough?

5. Did the speech have a definite opening, body and conclusion?

6. Did the speaker use notes effectively if she or he used notes?

7. What could the speaker have done differently that would have improved the speech?

8. What did you like about the speech?

9. Do you feel called to action or inspired by the speech?

If time permits, the group will discuss the speeches in general—what they liked and what they think could be improved next time.

Closure

The facilitator answers the question, "How do you feel you did?" Confirm the date, time, and place of the next meeting. Ask everyone to read the next module in the manual before the next meeting. Choose roles for the next meeting: host, facilitator, assistant facilitator, timekeeper, and recorder; make sure the facilitator and assistant facilitator have a copy of the Facilitation Guide to prepare. Ask participants to write anonymous feedback about the session before they leave. They can use the Feedback Form at the end of Module 1, or write whatever they like.

MODULE 4: FOR THE WELFARE OF THE EARTH AND ALL LIVING BEINGS

Objectives of Module 4

1. To understand the nature of pollution and climate change and how they impact people.
2. To realize the power of maximum utilization and rational distribution.
3. To understand the power of consciousness-raising groups and to learn how to form one of them.

Excitement Sharing

"What is something good that has happened in your life since we last met? Or would anyone like to read from your journal or share your recent activities?"

The Social Reality Discussion Question Pollution and Climate Change

Our question now is: What are your thoughts on the issues of pollution and climate change? How do they impact you? How do they make you feel?

We will go around the room, and ask everyone to say briefly what your thoughts are on the issues of pollution and climate change, and how they make you feel. Please speak for just one minute each.

[After everyone has spoken, 10-15 minutes] Excuse me, please, but we're going to stop this discussion now, only because, as usual in this course, we want to focus on the solutions.

Cooperative Game - Namaskar Game

"This next game involves no movement or touching, but is a very powerful non-judgmental reflection about who we are.

"First, I will teach you a greeting from India. Put your hands together and touch your thumbs to your forehead and then your heart. 'Namaskar' is a Sanskrit word which means, 'I greet the divinity within you with all my mind and all my heart.' Please repeat after me, 'Namaskar.' (Namaste is a variation of this Sanskrit word that is commonly used in Northwest India, and Namaskaram is the South India form.)

"We will do this exercise twice. Sit in pairs facing someone you don't know very well. One person of each pair has to close his or her eyes for three minutes. The second person will watch. Afterwards we will switch. Decide now who will be the first one to close their eyes." [Start soft music if you have it.]

"I will now give directions to the one whose eyes are open.

Look at the person in front of you. [pause] Imagine that this person is rather like you. [pause] Imagine that he or she has experienced some disappointments in life like you have. [pause] Imagine that he or she has made some mistakes in life like you have. [pause] Imagine that he or she has been hurt in life, sometimes physically, sometimes emotionally, just as you have. [pause] Imagine that because of these hurts, he or she has some worries and fears like you do. [pause] Imagine that he or she, like you, has also tried to be kind and to help people when possible. [pause] Imagine that he or she has some hopes and dreams like you have. [pause] Imagine that he or she would like to be a better person, just as you would like to be. [pause] Imagine that he or she has physical, mental and spiritual potential like you. [pause] Imagine that this person is profoundly beautiful inside, like you are. [pause] Now everyone, open your eyes, and put your hands together and touch your forehead and then touch your heart and say, 'Namaskar.'

"Now we will repeat, so those who were watching, now close your eyes and meditate; and those who were meditating, open your eyes." [repeat instructions]

It is better to read the instructions, so that both groups hear the very same words. After you have read the instructions twice, ask everyone to share with their partner for a couple of minutes what they experienced in this game. Then ask everyone to come into a circle.

You can explain that we are used to judging people a lot, even without knowing them ("he is bad," "she is good"), and that this exercise is designed to help us see another person without judgment, and to realize that everyone has good and bad within them, and the same physical, mental and spiritual potential we do. Prison inmates who do this are sometimes moved to tears. When we do this, we can overcome other emotions and feel forgiveness and compassion for the other person, as well as for ourselves, and finally unconditional love.

Did this game give you a feeling of compassion, and do you think it can awaken feelings of compassion in others? (15 minutes)

Prout's Vision Discussion Questions

Have you ever felt a personal sense of loss about the disappearance of a natural area, animals, or plants? If so, describe what happened and how you felt.

Worldwide 100 million people live within a meter (three feet) of sea level. Sea level rise associated with climate change could displace all of them. How will we resettle climate refugees?

Do you agree that Planet Earth and her wealth of resources are the common inheritance of all living beings? Why or why not?

Does consumerism bother you? Why or why not?

"Healthy individuals contribute to a healthy society, and a healthy society fosters the development of healthy individuals." Do you agree with this statement, and that individual interests and collective interests do not have to be in conflict?

Activist Tool Exercise Nature's Beauty, Loss, and Return

Let's do an exercise. Close your eyes for a few minutes and think about nature. Remember some happy times you've had in different places in nature. [pause] Remember some favorite places in nature that you experienced in your childhood and later in your adult life. [pause] Remember wild animals, fish, and birds you've encountered. [pause] Remember how good the natural world has made you feel at different times in your life. [pause] Now open your eyes. Would anyone like to briefly share some of your happy memories in nature? [Let participants share their feelings.]

It is said that we can't heal until we grieve. Please close your eyes again for a few minutes. Remember some natural places you've known that have been lost or polluted or damaged. [pause] Remember the ugly sights and smells of dead animals, trees, water and earth. [pause] Remember some tragic scenes you've seen or heard about. [pause] Become aware of how that environmental destruction makes you feel. [pause] Now open your eyes. Would anyone like to briefly share some of your grieving memories of nature? Please focus on your feelings. [Let participants share their feelings.]

Now place your hands on that part of your body where you feel the loss. Close your eyes for a moment and be aware of what you're feeling. [pause]

Now make a sound that expresses how you're feeling. [pause while everyone simultaneously makes sounds]

Now take a deep breath in and, as you breathe out, make the sound of a sigh. Let's do it again two more times together.

Close your eyes again. Imagine the energies of the earth and sky, all beings, all animals, all plants, with which we are connected. [pause] Imagine that beautiful energy of the universe grow and feel that energy surround you. [pause] Feel it wash away your grieving, like a cleansing bath. [pause] Imagine a beautiful light surrounding all of us so that we are collectively held. [pause] With your eyes still closed, imagine that it is fifty years from now. There is no more war or hunger or poverty. It is a world of peace and harmony with nature. We have stopped polluting the air and sea and land. A lot of reforestation has been done; the rivers are flowing clean again. Most of the endangered wildlife species have multiplied and are safe now. [pause]

Call out what that world looks like to you. [Let participants call out what they imagine.]

Open your eyes. Place your hands on that part of your body that is feeling this new world. What does that world feel like in your body? [Let participants express what it feels like to them.]

Imagine that hope and that vision is touching everyone. That beautiful vision means that people cannot help but get involved, infused with that possibility. Hundreds and thousands of people around the world are joining together with values of caring for one another and caring for the planet. How does that feel? [Let participants express what it feels like to them.]

Take a deep breath. Would you like to share how you felt about this consciousness-raising exercise? [Let participants express what it felt like to them.]

Joanna Macy has created many more and deeper practices to honor and grieve the Earth.

Closure

The facilitator answers the question, "How do you feel you did?" Confirm the date, time, and place of the next meeting. Ask everyone to read the next module in the manual before the next meeting. Choose roles for the next meeting: host, facilitator, assistant facilitator, timekeeper, and recorder; make sure the facilitator and assistant facilitator have a copy of the Facilitation Guide to prepare. Ask participants to write anonymous feedback about the session before they leave. They can use the Feedback Form at the end of Module 1, or write whatever they like.

MODULE 5: ETHICS FOR PERSONAL AND SOCIAL TRANSFORMATION

Objectives of Module 5

1. To understand the nature of crime and corruption and how they impact people.
2. To understand cardinal human values and ethics.
3. To understand the power of one-on-ones and to practice them.

Excitement Sharing

"What is something good that has happened in your life since we last met? Or would anyone like to read from your journal or share your recent activities?"

The Social Reality Discussion Question Corruption

Our question now is: What is your opinion of crime and corruption? How do they impact you? How do they make you feel?

We will go around the room, and ask everyone to say briefly what your opinion is of crime and corruption, and how they make you feel. Please speak for just one minute each.

[After everyone has spoken, 10-15 minutes] Excuse me, please, but we're going to stop this discussion now, only because, as usual in this course, we want to focus on the solutions.

Cooperative Game - Moral Dilemmas

"Sit in small groups of two or three. Each group should choose two of the following questions that have not been chosen by another group. Develop a collective answer to the questions, explaining your reasons. While the questions are simple, the answers often are not. Consider if your answer would change in different situations, and if so, why. It's important that every member of the group voice their opinion, because different people will think of different factors that might change your answer. Your goal is to reach consensus on your collective answers." (Different questions can be created for different societies.)

Is it all right to kill people?
Is it all right to kill animals?
Is it all right to fight for social justice?
Is it all right, if someone does wrong to you, to get revenge?
Is it all right to lie to avoid personal problems?
Is it all right to lie if it will help someone else?
Is it all right to criticize someone when they are not present?
Is it all right to cheat in school?

Is it all right to cheat on your partner?

Is it all right to accept a bribe?

Is it all right to give a bribe?

Is it all right to steal to help someone else?

Is it all right to accept a gift if it was stolen?

Is it all right to accept a donation if you are not sure where the money came from?

Is it all right to make as much money as you can?

Is it all right to spend a lot of money to throw a big party?

Is it all right to watch pornography?

Is it all right to earn money making pornography?

Is it all right to earn money selling alcohol and cigarettes?

Is it all right to earn money running a gambling casino?

Is it all right to consume whatever drugs you like?

Is it all right to earn money selling whatever drugs you like?

Is it all right to do whatever you want as long as no one finds out?

After every group has reported, "These questions are designed to elicit complex moral thinking. Our moral values should be like a compass that always points us in the right direction—would you agree with this? Why or why not?"

Prout's Vision Discussion Questions

What moral dilemmas does your country face today?

What moral dilemmas do you and your friends face today?

Do you know anyone who has the habit of lying? What are they like?

"Most moral values have reflected the interests of the rich and powerful." Do you agree with this statement? Give an example to support your view.

There is a cynical saying, "Everyone has their price," which means that a person who is able to resist a small temptation of money might give in if the amount is big enough. Have you ever seen an example of this?

Do you feel the ten universal ethical principles of Yama and Niyama could be a relevant guide to your actions today? Why or why not?

Have you ever met someone who claimed to be moral, but was not? How did their actions differ from their words?

Have you ever seen a government leader who claimed to be moral, but was not? How did their actions differ from their words?

"Accumulating as much money as you can is immoral." Do you agree? Why or why not?

"Pornography pollutes the mind." Do you agree? Why or why not?

Activist Tools Exercise One-on-Ones

1. Do a 20-minute interview with a participant you don't know very well. Usually one-on-ones go for about 45 minutes, so this is a shortened version. But you'd be amazed about how much information you can glean from 20 minutes.

2. Allow your partner to then do a 20-minute interview with you. Normally you wouldn't just switch roles like this; you'd give the person a chance to do a one-on-one with you at a different time if they wanted.

3. Talk a little about how you both thought the interviews went, and give each other any advice you might have.

Closure

The facilitator answers the question, "How do you feel you did?" Confirm the date, time, and place of the next meeting. Ask everyone to read the next module in the manual before the next meeting. Choose roles for the next meeting: host, facilitator, assistant facilitator, timekeeper, and recorder; make sure the facilitator and assistant facilitator have a copy of the Facilitation Guide to prepare. Ask participants to write anonymous feedback about the session before they leave. They can use the Feedback Form at the end of Module 1, or write whatever they like.

MODULE 6: A HEALTHY ECONOMY

Objectives of Module 6

1. To understand the nature of debt and how it impacts people.
2. To understand three-tiered economy.
3. To understand how to use winning words and slogans.

Excitement Sharing

"What is something good that has happened in your life since we last met? Or would anyone like to read from your journal or share your recent activities?"

The Social Reality Discussion Question Debt

Our question now is: What is your opinion about debt? Have you ever been in debt or witnessed it? How does it impact you? How does it make you feel?

We will go around the room, and ask everyone to say briefly what your opinion is about debt, and how it makes you feel. Please speak for just one minute each.

[After everyone has spoken, 10-15 minutes] Now let's shift our focus, because, as usual in this course, we want to focus on the solutions.

Cooperative Games - The Human Knot

If you have more than 14 people, divide into two groups. "Stand close together, shoulder-to-shoulder, and hold your arms straight out in front of you. Join each of your hands with the hands of two different people who are on the opposite side of the circle. Don't take the hand of someone standing beside you." [Pause while they do this.] "Got it? Congratulations, now you have created a human knot. The challenge is, without letting go of the hands you are holding, to untangle your knot. Start."

[After some hesitation, participants will start to duck under or step over the linked arms of others. Eventually the group should end up with one large circle of people holding hands, though some may be facing inwards and some outwards. Or there might be two interlocking circles, or even a circle within a circle. Occasionally a knot cannot be unraveled. In that case the leader can offer the technique used by Alexander the Great on the Gordian Knot: to use the proverbial sword to "cut" one link, freeing other hands and bodies that were blocked by it, and then at once to reconnect the link again. "Did the group become frustrated? If so, why? How did it feel when the group succeeded?"

Collective Back Massage: "Stand in a line, facing the back of the person in front of you. Put your hands on the shoulders of the person in front of you. If you have long hair, please move it over your shoulder and out of the way if you can. Close your eyes and imagine that there is a divine consciousness inside this person. Now put your hands together and touch your forehead and then touch your heart and say, 'Namaskar'. Give this person the best massage you've ever given to someone... Now turn around and say thank you." [15-20 minutes for both games.]

Prout's Vision Discussion Questions

A Prout slogan says, "Globalize humanity, localize the economy." How does a local economy compare with a global one? Is it possible to have both?

"It is a basic right of workers to own and manage their enterprises, making the economic decisions which directly affect their lives." Do you agree with this? Why or why not?

What has been your experience when you visit locally-owned businesses as compared with corporate-owned ones?

Activist Tools Exercise Winning Words Debate

We are going to have a short debate. There are two sides to every debate. In this debate the pro, or positive side, will assert the following proposition: Resolved: Our country should allow more immigrants to move here.

There will be two speakers on each team, the Pro Team and the Con Team, for a total of four in the debate. The two teams will have five minutes to discuss who will speak first and second and to plan a strategy to try to win the debate. Choose a timer, too.

The first speaker for the Pro Team explains in two minutes why more immigrants should be allowed to move here. Use as appealing words and images as possible. Remember that you want to appeal to the listeners' emotions. Describe the immigrants or refugees in a way that evokes compassion for them and values how much they can and do contribute to the country.

The first speaker for the Con Team speaks for two minutes in rebuttal to the first speaker by using emotional words to convince the audience that too many immigrants will hurt the country in different ways.

The second Pro Team member speaks for two minutes, followed by the second Con Team member for two minutes, both reasserting their arguments and rebutting the stances of the other team.

Final Closing Statements: One member for each team has just one minute to make their final closing remarks. No new ideas or facts can be presented in the closing statements.

At the end of the debate, decide which side's arguments were more effective. How were you affected by the words that each side chose to use about immigrants? What influenced you more, the logical arguments or the emotions stirred in you by the words and images used to depict immigrants? Why? Discuss the power of framing an argument with words that evoke positive or negative emotions in people.

Closure

The facilitator answers the question, "How do you feel you did?" Confirm the date, time, and place of the next meeting. Ask everyone to read the next module in the manual before the next meeting. Choose roles for the next meeting: host, facilitator, assistant facilitator, timekeeper, and recorder; make sure the facilitator and assistant facilitator have a copy of the Facilitation Guide to prepare. Ask participants to write anonymous feedback about the session before they leave. They can use the Feedback Form at the end of Module 1, or write whatever they like.

MODULE 7: COOPERATIVES CAN CREATE JOBS FOR ALL

Objectives of Module 7

1. To understand how unemployment impacts people.
2. To understand how cooperatives work.
3. To understand how to start a successful cooperative.

Excitement Sharing

"What is something good that has happened in your life since we last met? Or would anyone like to read from your journal or share your recent activities?"

The Social Reality Discussion Question Unemployment

Our question now is: What is your opinion about unemployment? How does it impact you? How does it make you feel?

We will go around the room, and ask everyone to say briefly what your opinion is about unemployment, and how it makes you feel. Please speak for just one minute each.

[After everyone has spoken, 10-15 minutes] Now let's shift our focus, because, as usual in this course, we want to focus on the solutions.

Cooperative Games - Cooperative Competition

This is done in pairs, face-to-face. One person stands with one foot forward and the other back; the partner touches their toes to the toes of the first person. Hold the hands in front of the shoulders, the right palm of the first person against the left palm of the partner, and match the other hands the same way. Then the two players push as hard as they can against each other in slow motion. Try to match one's strength with the strength of the partner, never allowing the partner to lose their balance and fall.

Variation: Stand back-to-back, feet apart, leaning against each other. Gradually, never breaking back contact, walk your feet in tiny steps away from each other until you are finally sitting back to back on the floor. Then walk yourselves back into a standing position.

Seesaw variation: "Sit on the floor facing your partner, with legs apart, knees bent. Your feet should be flat on the floor and near your partner's feet. Grab your partner's arms, not the hands. Then, like a cooperative seesaw, one starts to rise, pulled up by the other, and then starts to lower, pulling the partner up. You will always be part way up, like a seesaw.

At the end, "This is called cooperative competition because everyone is playing quite hard, and yet not trying to beat their opponent. Runners often find they run farther and faster when they have a somewhat evenly matched partner to practice with. Have you ever experienced a type of cooperative competition; if so, how did it feel?

"Did everyone act responsibly toward others in this game?

"Trust means to feel safe with, confident in and supported by the group. How much do you feel trust in this group?" [15 minutes.]

Prout's Vision Discussion Questions

"Cooperatives are the businesses of the future." Do you agree with this? Why or why not?

Have you ever visited or worked in a co-op? What impressed you most?

What factors do you think are most important for a co-op to be successful? Why?

If there was a credit union where you could keep your money instead of a commercial bank, would you use it?

Do you think your community would benefit if it had more co-ops? Why or why not?

Activist Tools Exercise Create a Co-op!

Brainstorm together and make a list of goods and services that are needed in your community that a co-op might provide. Consider basic necessities, transportation, agriculture and agricultural products, expensive imported goods that could be produced locally, cleaning, consulting, computer services, pest control, etc.

Next, choose any product or service from your list to collectively consider. How many members would ideally begin this co-op? What kind of location would be needed to start? What materials and inventory would be needed to start? What competitive advantages would your product or service have in the market? How much money would be needed at the beginning, and when could you expect to start making a profit? What is your plan for growth? What sources might provide the funding you need? How many jobs could your co-op eventually provide?

Closure

The facilitator answers the question, "How do you feel you did?" Confirm the date, time, and place of the next meeting. Ask everyone to read the next module in the manual before the next meeting. Choose roles for the next meeting: host, facilitator, assistant facilitator, timekeeper, and recorder; make sure the facilitator and assistant facilitator have a copy of the Facilitation Guide to prepare. Ask participants to write anonymous feedback about the session before they leave. They can use the Feedback Form at the end of Module 1, or write whatever they like.

MODULE 8: FOOD FOR ALL

Objectives of Module 8

1. To understand the nature of hunger and how it impacts people.
2. To understand how agriculture works.
3. To understand how to create media impact.

Excitement Sharing

"What is something good that has happened in your life since we last met? Or would anyone like to read from your journal or share what happened in your recent activities?"

The Social Reality Discussion Question Hunger

Our question now is: What is your opinion about hunger? How does it impact you? How does it make you feel?

We will go around the room, and ask everyone to say briefly what your opinion is about hunger, and how it makes you feel. Please speak for just one minute each.

[After everyone has spoken, 10-15 minutes] Now let's shift our focus because, as usual in this course, we want to focus on the solutions.

Cooperative Game - When Will Hunger, Poverty and War End?

Before the participants arrive, lay a strip of adhesive tape across the floor of the room. If the room is carpeted, you can use a string instead. If necessary, it also works to just use an imaginary line. If you use masking tape, write "Now" at one end, "100+" at the other end, and "50" in the middle. Then write "10," "20," etc. so the tape becomes a timeline between now and 100+ years in the future.

"I would like to ask each of you, 'When do you think hunger, poverty and war will end?' I believe none of us really knows the answer to that question. Yet, I believe that reflecting on this question and our beliefs about changing the world for the better has value. So I would like each of you to stand near the point of the timeline that represents your guess as to when you think it might happen. When you are all standing where you want to be, on behalf of 'Prout TV,' I will begin asking people where you are standing, meaning when you think it will happen, and why you believe that. Of course every answer is correct, because you are stating your honest opinion."

Holding either a real microphone or a pretend one, start at the far end, 100+ years, and ask the first person in a loud voice so everyone can hear, "Where are you standing, madam, and why?" Slowly move your way down the line toward the present.

After you are finished, say, "Next I would like to ask each of you to stand by the point on the timeline when you *want* hunger, poverty and war to end." [laughter, as everyone moves down to 'Now.']

"All right, it's good to know we all agree that we want hunger, poverty and war to end now. My next question is, 'What could we do to make that great day come sooner?'"

To conclude, remind the group that thinking about the future has value, because it helps us know what we want for the world, what might be possible and what we can do now to help create our ideal future.

"Within each person is room for hope. Did this game increase your hope for the future? How?"

"Do we need to feel hope in order to act? Why?" [15 minutes.]

Prout's Vision Discussion Questions

How much of the food that you eat is grown locally, and how much is imported from far away?

Do you think an agrarian revolution is necessary? Why or why not?

Have you ever visited a cooperative farm, a Community Supported Agriculture farm, a permaculture project, an ecovillage, or a Transition Town? If so, what was it like?

"Since 1950, the number of farm animals on the planet has risen 500 percent; now they outnumber humans by ten to one, consume half the world's grain, and cause more global warming than all cars and other transportation put together." What is your opinion about this?

Have you ever eaten food that you planted yourself? How did it make you feel?

Activist Tools Exercise Plan a Media Event

First, choose a cause that is dear to you, whether local or global. Then brainstorm together for ten minutes how you could get local media coverage for this cause.

Brainstorming is a group creativity technique to generate new ideas and solutions by removing inhibitions. People are able to think more freely and they suggest as many spontaneous new ideas as possible. Every idea is noted down as fast as possible. No criticism of any idea is allowed, no matter how wild it may be. In fact, wild ideas are encouraged as they stimulate other creative solutions.

After the 10-minute time limit is over, stop the brainstorm, and begin evaluating as a group each of the proposals. Feel free to combine and modify proposals in this phase. Try to reach consensus on which idea could generate the most positive local media coverage for your cause.

Finally, most challenging of all, do it!

Closure

The facilitator answers the question, "How do you feel you did?" Confirm the date, time, and place of the next meeting. Ask everyone to read the next module in the manual before the next meeting. Choose roles for the next meeting: host, facilitator, assistant facilitator, timekeeper, and recorder; make sure the facilitator and assistant facilitator have a copy of the Facilitation Guide to prepare. Ask participants to write anonymous feedback about the session before they leave. They can use the Feedback Form at the end of Module 1, or write whatever they like.

MODULE 9: IDEAL LEADERSHIP

Objectives of Module 9

1. To understand the nature of poor leaders and how they impact people.
2. To understand classes based on social psychology.
3. To understand the Social Cycle and Sadvipras.
3. To understand how to become an ideal leader.

Excitement Sharing

"What is something good that has happened in your life since we last met? Or would anyone like to read from your journal or share your recent activities?"

The Social Reality Discussion Question Dangerous Leaders

Our question now is: Have you ever met a dangerous leader? If so, what were they like? How did they make you feel? What effect did they have on their organization?

We will go around the room, and ask everyone to say briefly what your opinion is about bad leaders, and how they make you feel. Please speak for just one minute each.

[After everyone has spoken, 10-15 minutes] Now let's shift our focus, because, as usual in this course, we want to focus on the solutions.

Cooperative Game – The Sarkar Game

Before the game, print enough copies of the scripts below so that every participant gets a copy of the script for their group. Divide all the participants into four equal groups. Gather work tools (hammers, screwdrivers, brooms, etc.) for the first group; ideally, one tool for each member of that group. Give toy guns or large kitchen knives to the second group, books to the third group, and credit cards and play money to the fourth. A bell, whistle, or red flag for the facilitator to get everyone's attention is optional.

"Prabhat Ranjan Sarkar's theory of the Social Cycle shows the different ways that humans have dealt with their physical environment and with one another through both individual and collective psychology.

"Read your script and play just that role. Please remember that there are both positive and negative aspects of your archetype. Be aware of both potentials as you interact with others. Take a few minutes to discuss in your group what you want to do." [Give everyone five to ten minutes to plan.]

Below are the written instruction scripts to be handed to each group:

Group 1, Workers: You work hard and take pride in doing a good job. You are preoccupied with survival and mundane pleasures. You tend to trust and support your fellow workers. You want safety, security and reasonable comforts. You want inspiration and faith to ease suffering and the fear of death. TV, a cold beer, sex, and watching sports are common pastimes. You usually leave complex political and economic decisions to leaders you trust. When inspired, you loyally follow leaders of the other classes. But if your needs are not met, you can disrupt, create chaos, or even bring the system down. Your group will begin the game. So prepare a simple skit lasting a couple of minutes or so, revealing your nature until the other groups enter and interact with you. Remember there are both positive and negative aspects of your archetype. Use your imagination and speak loudly and clearly.

Group 2, Warriors: Your physical strength and courage are your greatest assets. You embrace challenge and struggle. You value honor, discipline, and self-sacrifice. Your will, patience, and hard work are your strengths. You protect society from danger and chaos, by enforcing order. The military, police, firefighting, and rescue teams are your chosen work. Sports and martial arts are your hobbies. You obey and expect others to obey authority and follow orders, no matter what. Your group will be the second group to enter the game. Decide how you will interact with the first group of workers. Remember there are both positive and negative aspects of your archetype. Use your imagination and speak loudly and clearly.

Group 3, Intellectuals: Your developed mind is your greatest asset. The search for truth, removing errors and confusion, is your purpose. Some of you have knowledge of science, while others have knowledge of spiritual reality. You protect everyone by making rules and laws and commanding the warriors to enforce them. You debate hard so that the best ideas win. You create enlightenment. The arts are your hobbies. You lead others by establishing your religion, your science, or your political system as the Truth. Your group will be the third group to enter the game. Decide how you will interact with the groups of workers and warriors. Remember there are both positive and negative aspects of your archetype. Use your imagination and speak loudly and clearly.

Group 4, Merchants: You make money easily and invest it wisely. You excel in organizing and running companies. Efficient and effective, you manage large numbers of people to make new products and carry out difficult tasks. Through wealth and power, you can help everyone. You reward loyal service with higher salaries. Efficiency is very important. Your group will be the last group to enter the game. Decide how you will interact with the groups of workers, warriors and intellectuals. Remember there are both positive and negative aspects of your archetype. Use your imagination and speak loudly and clearly.

Facilitation Tips: This is an action learning process that introduces participants to the Social Cycle and its holistic perspective of social change. Invite the workers to begin their role play and the other groups to observe until called in. After two or three minutes, invite the warriors to enter. When you feel that perverse behaviors are present or the game is going flat, stop the play and ask the intellectuals to enter. Allow the three-part dynamic to continue until the behavior again becomes perverse, and then the merchants are invited in. When all the groups have had their chance to dominate, stop the game.

Then ask everyone to sit down but to stay in their groups. Debrief each group in turn, with everyone listening. Ask one member to read their script aloud. Then ask the group to describe how they tried to act out their role, and ask the other groups for their opinions. Build a dynamic picture of each group. Highlight the healthy form of each class, and how each group wins power in a beneficial phase. Point out, too, the inherent suffering that each group in the end creates in its perverse phase. Even though each class succeeds in managing problems, it also contains the seeds of its ultimate decline. It is important for people to remember that all four classes exist in each society.

We all have deep scripts that tell us about roles, power, and relationships in the world. These scripts have been programmed into us and continue to direct us unconsciously until an experience makes us aware of them. This game creates an experience of social change that is, at its heart, revolutionary.

Once the nature of social change is clear, you can then introduce the idea of an invisible fifth force in the room. Conscious of the strengths and weaknesses of each group, one can choose to personally develop all four abilities and become a spiritual revolutionary. [20 minutes.]

Prout's Vision Discussion Questions

Which qualities of the four classes (laborer, warrior, intellectual, and merchant) have you developed in your life? What would it take to develop the others?

According to the theory of the Social Cycle, which class is dominating your society now, and what would it take to move it forward?

Do you think that anyone could become an ideal leader, a sadvipra? Why or why not?

"One's universal outlook is a way to judge whether a person is a sadvipra." Is your outlook completely universal, or do you harbor negative feelings about any group of people?

"True leaders empower others to be great. They sincerely listen to the opinions of others, and they encourage and praise the accomplishments of others." Do you?

"What we despise in others—the qualities that we hate—are actually within us." What qualities do you hate in other people? Are those qualities also within you?

Have you ever met someone who was "emotionally intelligent:" sensitive, aware, and always able to make others feel better?

Have you ever met someone you consider to be a true hero? What were they like?

Activist Tools Exercise The Great Game of Power by Augusto Boal

This game helps us understand how power is created, perceived, and experienced in different situations.

Arrange a table, six identical chairs and a bottle at the front of the room. Ask a volunteer to come forward and silently arrange the objects so as to make one chair become the most powerful object, in relation to the other chairs, the table and the bottle. Any of the objects can be placed on top of one another, or on their sides, or whatever, but none of the objects can be removed from the space.

Everyone is invited to analyze which chair has the most power while the person who made the arrangement keeps quiet. Ask, "What real life situation does this image represent? Why? What else could it be?" The diverse experiences and beliefs of each person will color their decisions and perspectives. Remember, there is no right answer.

Next invite another person to silently arrange the objects. Many variations should result. Then the group could choose one arrangement in which one chair is clearly more powerful. Invite a person to enter the scene without moving anything and position their own body so they have the most power. Once someone is in place, the other members of the group can enter the space in succession and try to place themselves in an even more powerful position, and take away the power the first person had.

Reflection: What are some of the different ways we saw power in this game? What makes someone or something powerful? Who or what is powerful in our world today? Why? (Boal 2002)

MODULE 10: NEOHUMANISM

Objectives of Module 10

1. To understand the nature of media lies and how they impact people.
2. To understand what is neohumanism.
3. To understand how to use critical study to understand privilege.

Excitement Sharing

"What is something good that has happened in your life since we last met? Or would anyone like to read from your journal or share your recent activities?"

The Social Reality Discussion Question Media Lies

Our question now is: Have you ever felt subjected to media lies? If so, what were they like? How did they make you feel?

We will go around the room, and ask everyone to say briefly what your opinion is about media lies, and how they make you feel. Please speak for just one minute each.

[After everyone has spoken, 10-15 minutes] Now let's shift our focus, because, as usual in this course, we want to focus on the solutions.

Cooperative Game – Prejudice

Participants stand in a line at one side of the room. Ask the participants to walk to a selected area about three meters (ten feet) away if they would answer 'yes' to the following question:

"Have you ever been treated differently because of your gender?"

Then invite each person who answered yes to tell the context of how and where it happened, and how it made them feel. Then all of them should walk back to the starting line to listen to the next question.

"Have you ever treated people differently because of your gender?" Those who answer 'yes' walk to the other place, explain the context and answer, "What was that like and how did it make you feel?"

"Have you ever been treated differently because of your skin color?" [pause] "What was that like and how did it make you feel?"

"Have you ever treated people differently because of their skin color?" [pause] "What was that like and how did it make you feel?"

"Have you ever been treated differently because of your nationality or religion?" [pause] "What was that like and how did it make you feel?"

"Have you ever been treated differently based on your clothes, hairstyle, body piercings, tattoos or anything else in your appearance?" [pause] "What was that like and how did it make you feel?"

"Have you ever been treated differently due to your age?"

"Have you ever treated people differently due to their age?"

"Are there any other related questions that should be asked?"

[Note: The way the first question is worded may lead men, as well as women, to answer 'yes', if they are aware of their privilege, an "invisible package of unearned assets," such as having access to higher education, gaining psychological self-confidence, or having a sense of belonging or worth in society. In the same way, members of the majority race, religion, etc., may answer 'yes' to all the questions due to the deference they are shown and the social connections afforded them.] Afterwards, ask the group the following questions:

How did it feel to stand apart from the group because you have been treated differently?

Does prejudice still exist in this society? What is the root cause of prejudice?

What could be done to dispel stereotypes and prejudicial attitudes? What could you do personally to dispel stereotypes and prejudicial attitudes? [20 minutes. Source: Matt Oppenheim, PhD.]

Prout's Vision Discussion Questions

Have you ever experienced dogma, geo-sentiment or socio-sentiment? Describe the situation.

In your opinion, is there a lack of social and economic awareness among the people of your country? If so, why?

Are fear and inferiority complexes imposed on people in your country? If so, how?

Have you ever experienced racism directly or indirectly? Describe your experience.

Have you ever experienced exploitation directly or indirectly? Describe your experience.

Are lotteries legal in your country? Should they be? Why or why not?

Pseudo-culture means that which is fake, imposed, which has a debilitating effect psychologically and spiritually and which lowers the will of people to resist. Can you give examples of pseudo-culture in your society? How can we decide what is true culture and what is fake?

Do advertisements in your country make young people want to be someone else? Explain.

How many popular songs do you know that inspire people to rise up and make a revolution? What percentage of pop stars do you know that are revolutionary role models? Why don't more do this?

What percentage of popular TV shows do you know that inspire people to rise up and make a revolution? Why don't more do this?

Activist Tools Exercise Mapping Difference

Have each person identify their ethnic background, race, gender, sexual orientation, educational background, religious or spiritual background, economic class (upper class, middle class, working class, other), age, marital and parental status, and whether or not they are disabled in some way. [After everyone has done this.] "You will probably feel that this exercise does not reveal very much about who you really are: your personal story, your character, your hopes and feelings. However, this wheel of diversity says a lot about the social reality that has influenced you during your lifetime. Imagine how your life would change if you suddenly had a different skin color, or a different gender, or a different sexual orientation, or if you were deaf or blind. How would people treat you differently? What opportunities would open or close to you?"

Closure

The facilitator answers the question, "How do you feel you did?" Ask the group what they would like to do now that the course is over. Ask participants to write anonymous feedback about the session before they leave. They can use the Feedback Form at the end of Module 1, or write whatever they like. Please fill out the Course Evaluation Feedback, too.

Course Evaluation: Feedback on Group Process

If you were part of a Tools to Change the World Study Circle, in addition to filling out the Course Evaluation at the end of the manual, we would love to hear from one representative about the group. Please fill out this group evaluation at https://prout.info/group-evaluation. Or mail it to us at Dada Maheshvarananda, 6 Breyerton Court, Asheville, NC 28804, USA. Thank you for your participation.

The Group

1) Where did this group meet? Please list place, city, state or province, and country _____
_____

2) What publicity was done to find enough participants? How successful was it?_____
_____

3) When did the first meeting and the last meeting take place? _____

4) How many modules did the group do? _____

5) How many participants attended at least one session? _____

6) How many of them were under 25 years of age___? From 25 to 50 ___? Over 50 ___?

7) How many participants attended at least five sessions? _____

8) How many participants attended at least nine sessions? _____

9) Do you feel confident enough and interested enough to organize another course? Why or why not? _____

CPSIA information can be obtained
at www.ICGtesting.com
Printed in the USA
LVHW061915140922
728365LV00004B/16